THOUGHTS ON STEWARDSHIP
Volume One

by
Rodney M. Howard-Browne

R.H.B.E.A. Publications
Louisville, Kentucky

Thoughts on Stewardship, Volume One
ISBN 1-884662-00-5
Copyright © 1993 by
Rodney M. Howard-Browne
P.O. Box 197161
Louisville, KY 40259-7161 U.S.A.

Published by
R.H.B.E.A. Publications
P.O. Box 197161, Louisville, KY 40259-7161 U.S.A.
P.O. Box 3900, Randburg 2125 South Africa

CONTENTS

ACKNOWLEDGEMENT

Special thanks to my good friends Norman and Eleanor Robertson for all of their hard work in helping with the compilation of these thirteen teachings to complete Volume One. You have been a great blessing.

INTRODUCTION

It is more blessed to give than to receive.   Acts 20:35

A key aspect of our revivals which has supernaturally blessed thousands of believers and impacted hundreds of local churches in the United States, South Africa, Europe and Australia is our teaching on stewardship.

At each service, before we receive the offering, I always share practical insights from God's Word concerning the plan and purpose of God to bless His people financially. Wherever we minister, we constantly receive good reports of God's financial provision in the lives of Christians. Pastors also report that the income of their local church has increased by as much as fifty to sixty percent.

Because of this and by the request of many pastors, I felt led by God to put these Christian principles of financial steward-ship into print, *Thoughts on Stewardship*, Volume One, Volume Two, Volume Three and Volume Four.

I know this book will greatly bless you and it is my prayer that every pastor will boldly teach and share these insights with his congregation and that every Christian will boldly act upon these principles and thereby walk in God's abundant blessings!

Sincerely in Christ,

Rodney M. Howard-Browne

5

1

PROSPERITY GOD'S WAY

Beloved, I pray that you may prosper in every way and (that your body) may keep well, even as (I know) your soul keeps well and prospers.

In fact I greatly rejoice when (some of) the brethren from time to time arrived and spoke (so highly) of the sincerity and fidelity of your life, as indeed you do live in the Truth (the whole Gospel presents).

3 John 2,3 (Amplified)

I enjoy reading the Scriptures in the amplified version because the truths contained in them seem to come across a little louder and clearer. Every promise that God has given us has a condition attached to it. Many times we don't read the Word in the context in which it was written. So, in order to find out what God is talking about in the above verses, we need to read on.

I have no greater joy than this, to hear that my (spiritual) children are living their lives in the Truth.

Beloved....

Are you the beloved of the Lord?

... it is a fine and faithful work that you are doing when you give any service to the (Christian) brethren, and (especially when they are) strangers.

3 John 4, 5 (Amplified)

Honor Your Word, God Honors His

In the book of Hebrews, we are told to be careful when we entertain strangers, **for some have entertained angels unawares** (Heb. 13:2). Sometimes, it is easy to be hospitable to the people we know. It is easy to be charming and say, "Y'all come by and see us." But when "Y'all come by and see us," you wonder, "Why did they come by?" I didn't really mean that literally, it was just a greeting.

Some people are very diplomatic. They have sharpened the art of diplomacy. Do you know what that means? The person who is diplomatic has the ability to tell somebody to go to hell in such a way that they look forward to the trip! Many people are in the habit of telling others something, but then, when they are called up on it, they aren't too happy about it. Next time, don't promise something you're not going to fulfill. Don't try to be charming and nice, and promise people things that you're not going to do. If you can't believe your own word, why should you believe God's Word?

Again, it's easy to be charming and entertain people you know. But the Bible talks about being hospitable and going out of your way to help people, perhaps strangers. Putting yourself out to help others.

God Always Takes Care of Us

There were times in the past when my wife and I really didn't even have much food. At the same time we had members of our family who were in need, but we took them in, anyway. We put them up in a room and fed them. And you know, the week we did that, extra food came in and God took care of us. The fact is that when we stretch ourselves to take care of others, the supply just increases.

In 1985 we left the church we were pastoring in the southern part of our country, South Africa, because we thought we were coming to America. We gave away everything we owned — even all the furniture. Then, God said, "No. It isn't time yet," and He moved us onto the staff of a very large church. Because of our change of circumstances we moved into an apartment and had nothing — not one bit of furniture.

We were planning to sleep on the floor the first night we moved into the apartment. Then, I heard a knock on the door. It was a minister friend of mine. He said, "Look, we have these double bunks and they'll be good for the kids. They have just been sitting in our garage. They are like new, but we can't use them. Would you like them?" I said, "The kids would like them." We were the kids who slept very comfortably that first night!

The way in which God furnished that apartment was just supernatural. We saw an advertisement in the newspaper for a double bed. We phoned the people and they came to the house. While we were talking, the power of God hit the guy and he started weeping and crying. He said, "I can't sell this bed to you, I'm giving it to you. You have to take it." And this is how everything came in. God is true to His Word.

I am sharing the miraculous provision of God because our family has experienced it firsthand and I want you to be encouraged. We know His Word is true; we have stood on these truths and God has always come through. God watches over His Word to perform it. Do you ever wonder if God is concerned with your daily needs? The answer is yes.

God's Supernatural Provision

When we first moved to America, we didn't have a vehicle or, for that matter, anything else. We couldn't get credit any-

9

where. If you have never moved to a new country, you don't know what it's like. You just can't get credit. I would go to a department store and say, "Could I open an account here?" The answer was, "Sorry, do you have any credit?" Then, I would say, "No. But if you don't let me open an account, how in the world am I going to get a credit history?" So, I would walk the entire shopping mall and pick up applications from every store. I just kept filling them out — one a week — until they felt so sorry for me, I had cards coming from everywhere. That is how we built credit. It took us about three years.

As my ministry was just starting in America, I remember having to leave my family in Louisville, where our offices were located, and flying in and out continuously. I did this for seven months. Finally, I said, "I'm not doing that anymore." So I started taking them on the road with me. Prior to this time, while I was on the road, my wife was by herself taking care of our three small children — at the time, Kirsten was five, Kelly three and Kenneth only eight months old. She would have to walk through the snow with all of them to the laundromat to wash clothes. You must understand that when you come from Africa where you *never* see snow, walking through a little bit of snow is like going through the North Pole — it's a blizzard. It's a traumatic experience.

My wife told me, "I can't take walking through the snow with all the children." Well, I didn't know what I was going to do because we didn't have a vehicle. We had nothing. She had to walk to the store, the laundromat and everywhere. One day she said, "I'm going to go out and just buy a washer and dryer." I said, "No, just wait a few days. I'm praying and we are going to get them. You don't have to buy them." I didn't go around and tell everybody about it.

Some people think that faith without "hints" is dead. They go down to the altar and pray in a loud voice, "Lord, thou knowest that I need, oh God, a washer and dryer." And then, the brothers and sisters feel sorry for them, so they help them.

They say, "Oh, isn't God wonderful, He met my need." Yeah, because they opened their big mouth.

The very next week, my wife went to church and a lady walked up to her and said, "Maybe I'm out of place asking this, but do you have a washer and dryer?" Of course, my wife said, "No." So the lady said to her, "My mother just bought me a brand new set and mine are pretty new, but I can't have two sets. You can have the extra one. Will that be all right?" My wife brought them to the house and they even matched the colors of our kitchen. God's provision has always been there.

He Wants To Meet Your Every Need

Don't ever think that God isn't concerned with your daily life, because He is. Don't you think that God wants to bless His children? Let me ask you a question. If Jesus came to your house tonight, do you think He would meet your needs? The news I have for you is that Jesus has already come to your house. He wants to bless you. He wants to meet your every need. He wants to take care of you.

When Jesus and the disciples needed money to pay taxes, Jesus told them to go fishing. When they needed food, there was a little boy's lunch. When they ran out of wine at the wedding of Canaan, He turned the water into wine. When He needed transportation, He told His disciples to go to "Levi and Sons" donkey dealerships and tell Mr. Levi, "My master has need of that new donkey — that one on the showroom floor." He met every need.

God is speaking to His people today. He is telling us that we can't just look at the natural. If God has His eye on the sparrow, how much more will He watch over you? He cares for the lily of the field, the birds of the air. How much more will He provide for you? Are you not much better than a bird? (Matt. 6:26,28.)

Give and It Shall Be Given Unto You

They have testified before the church, of your love and friendship. You will do well to forward them on their journey (and you will please do so) in a way worthy of God's (service).

3 John 6 (Amplified)

Have you ever wondered how people would treat Jesus if they knew He was going to their house tonight? If we would just treat each other the way we would treat Jesus, we would not have any problems.

These (traveling missionaries) have gone out for the Name's sake (for His sake) and are accepting nothing from the Gentiles (the heathen, the non-Israelites).

3 John 7 (Amplified)

When we came to America, we were not approached by a large beer company that said, "Brother Rodney, we just love your ministry. We believe in what it stands for — people getting drunk on the new wine. We want you to know that we are sponsoring you to the tune of $150,000 a year." We were not approached by a large hotel chain that said, "We really believe in your ministry. Wherever you go in the United States, you can stay free of charge. We were not approached by a large restaurant chain where we were sponsored with free food. No, the heathen have done absolutely nothing. We were not approached by Jerry the Rat and Four Fingers Brown. "Hey, Brother Rodney, we believe in this ministry. Me and my cousin Joey were talking about getting behind it." No, the Mafia didn't approach us.

It is clear that the heathen don't support God's work. The support comes from God's people. We do not solicit funds through the mail at all. For us, this makes Scriptural sense. God has never failed us. We felt that in ten years time, we did not want to end up in "Prison Ministries International" for not being good stewards over our finances. So the way we receive our offerings is by giving the Word of God — not by using gimmicks, not under pressure. We receive our provision by just obeying the Holy Spirit and the Word of God.

Somebody says, "Why should I give?" I'm glad you asked.

So we ourselves ought to support such people (to welcome and provide for them), in order that we may be fellow workers in the Truth (the whole Gospel) and cooperate with its teachers.

3 John 8 (Amplified)

That's why you should give. So that you can become a fellow worker in the truth and cooperate with its teachers. What people don't understand is that when they sow financially, their money doesn't die in the offering basket. That's actually the ground in which they plant their seed. The place where you plant your seed is vital. You might not see that return the next day or the next week, but you *will* see the return.

There is an eternal harvest that is accumulating to your account. We have had great revivals in three cities in Alaska — Ketchikan, Juneau and Anchorage. This revival has swept even into the remote parts of Alaska. I believe that to those of you who have supported this ministry, the Lord will show the Alaskan people who have been touched, when you get to heaven. You will say, "God, I never went to Alaska." God will say, "No, you didn't, but do you remember that crazy African preacher who came through town and whom you supported? He went there and those are the souls that were won. They come to your account." That is how it works.

God has made abundant provision for all your needs. Get a hold of the truths contained in His Word and apply them to your life. Remember that God is the original Jew and that He keeps a very accurate accounting system. He knows exactly how to account — not one dime goes misplaced. Trust in Him and you will see His abundant provision.

2

BLESSED OR CURSED — IT'S UP TO YOU

I call heaven and earth as witnesses today against you, that I have set before you life and death, blessing and cursing; therefore choose life, that both you and your descendants may live.

Deuteronomy 30:19

Deuteronomy 28 lists the blessings and the cursings given by God to the Israelites under the Old Covenant. When you read this chapter, you probably have the same feelings I do. I really don't want to read the cursings. The blessings, however, I do want to read because if we remember,

Christ has redeemed us from the curse of the law, having become a curse for us (for it is written, "Cursed is everyone who hangs on a tree"), that the blessing of Abraham might come upon the Gentiles in Christ Jesus, that we may receive the promise of the Spirit through faith. And if you are Christ's, then you are Abraham's seed, and heirs according to the promise.

Galatians 3:13,14,29

15

A New Commandment

If we read through the first five books of the Bible, the Pentateuch, we find out the curse of the law was three fold — poverty, sickness and spiritual death. Through Christ, we have been redeemed from the law. God has provided for us, His children, abundance instead of poverty, divine healing and health instead of sickness, and eternal life instead of spiritual death. As Christians, we don't have to keep the law. We don't have to live by the ten commandments because Jesus said, **A new commandment I give to you, that you love one another** (John 14:34).

So in reality, there are no longer ten commandments, there's only one, because everything is wrapped up into that one commandment. If you love one another, you won't rob, you won't steal, you won't murder. All the law is fulfilled in that one commandment.

When God's commandments were enforced and followed in the Old Testament, God's blessings came upon the people. How much more under the New Covenant which is based upon better promises, signed and sealed with the Blood of Jesus? If we keep His commandment to love, His blessings are going to be poured upon us.

I don't think I have ever met a poor Jew. Obviously, there are some who are not walking according to the Covenant, but everywhere I go I find that the Jewish people have risen up and prospered because they have been taught the Law — they know the blessings and they know the cursings.

Overtaken by the Blessings of God

Do you want to be overtaken by the blessings? Let's examine and read carefully what Deuteronomy 28 says about it.

And all these blessings shall come upon you and overtake

you, because you obey the voice of the Lord your God.

Blessed shall you be in the city, and blessed shall you be in the country. Blessed shall be the fruit of your body, the produce of your ground and the increase of your herds, the increase of your cattle and the offspring of your flocks.

Blessed shall be your basket and your kneading bowl. Blessed shall you be when you come in, and blessed shall you be when you go out. The Lord will cause your enemies who rise against you to be defeated before your face; they shall come out against you one way and flee before you seven ways.

The Lord will command the blessing on you in your storehouses and in all to which you set your hand, and He will bless you in the land which the Lord your God is giving you.

The Lord will open to you His good treasure, the heavens, to give the rain to your land in its season, and to bless all the work of your hand. You shall lend to many nations, but you shall not borrow.

And the Lord will make you the head and not the tail; you shall be above only, and not be beneath, if you heed the commandments of the Lord your God, which I command you today, and are careful to observe them.

Deuteronomy 28:2-8,12,13

And then you can read on, **Cursed shall you be in the city and the field...** (Deut. 28:16-68). The remaining verses in the chapter talk about some of the most horrifying things you have ever heard. Terrible actions are described — even people who ate their children because the city had been seized and their food ran out. These are the types of actions taking place in countries where God isn't honored — where His commandments have not been followed.

Do you know why America has been blessed? Because America was founded on Christian principles. It's not that way today, but the seed is still manifesting itself. The devil can't just uproot the good spiritual foundation that this country had. I am sorry to say this, but today America is not a Christian nation, although its Godly roots are still here.

If you travel to other countries, you will find that their people worship so many different gods. For example, the nation of India has over three hundred million gods — and it is also a poverty-stricken country. As a rule, the less a country has of God, the more intense the poverty. Why? Because poverty is a curse. Wherever the devil is manifested, there is poverty.

Poverty Is Not a Virtue

Unfortunately, the Church has said for so long that poverty is a virtue. If you believe God's Word, then you should believe that poverty is a curse not a virtue. Poverty doesn't come from heaven above. It comes from hell beneath.

If you were raised in a home where there was a "poverty mentality" or a "sickness mentality" most likely you have been affected by it. You have to stand up and rebuke it. If you don't, you will be like so many people who are saved but who suffer in poverty and disease — sometimes most of their lives.

All because they have not come to the realization that their healing has been purchased for them on the cross of Calvary by the stripes that Jesus bore. Therefore, they haven't stood up and enforced the devil's defeat concerning sickness and disease. They haven't said, "I will walk in God's healing power. I will have God's healing power in my body." This concept applies to all of God's blessing. We must realize that Jesus is not only our Savior, He is also our Healer and Provider. He will make sure His promises are fulfilled.

We must stand up and say, "I'm going to appropriate the promises of God today in Jesus' name. I take authority over poverty. I take authority over the mentality of poverty in

Jesus' name. Satan, you will have no part of me, my spouse or my children. You will have no part of my family. My seed and I are going to be blessed because we serve and obey God."

The Scriptures say that if we obey Him, we will spend our years in prosperity and our days in pleasure. (Job 36:11.) God wants us to understand this truth. Some people get angry when I teach on this subject. But we need to remember that it is the religious spirit that is getting angry because the devil wants to keep people in bondage and make them think they are serving God. Satan wants you to think you are pleasing God, when in reality he is robbing you of the blessing of the Word of God.

Hide God's Word in Your Heart

Knowing that God wants to meet your needs is not enough. You have to stand on the Word of God, you have to appropriate His promises on a daily basis. You have to take God's Word and hide it in your heart.

If you are a young couple just starting your married life, you need to declare the provision God has made for you. You need to say, "Poverty will be far from us. We're not going to have it in our house. It's not going to affect our children." This is how you can set the course of your life.

The decisions that you make today will affect you in the years to come. You follow God's direction when you base your beliefs on the Word of God and on your obedience to His commandment. This is pleasing in His sight and the blessings of God will come upon you as a result. Don't just accept poverty in your life. Get angry about it and rebuke it. Remember the importance of not violating the principles that God has given us in His Word. As you walk in His blessings, obey the voice of the Spirit of God and He will lead you in the way that He wants you to go.

God Wants To Bless You

If you want to receive the blessings of God in your life, you'd better work. I like what D. L. Moody said, "I get down and pray like it all depends on God and then I get up and go like it all depends on me." God can only bless a moving ship. But those who are anchored in the dry docks of indecision are going nowhere. The Word of God isn't going to line up with your circumstances. Your circumstances must line up with the Word of God. He has made provision for us. Everything that God has for us is available through His Word.

Resist the Spirit of Poverty

Don't let anybody tell you that you might be ruined by prosperity. The Bible says that prosperity only ruins the fool. If your heart is right, then you can be blessed by God so you can be made a blessing unto man. So let your prayer be, "I'm not a fool. I hear God's Word and apply it to my life. I base what I believe on the Word of God, not upon my circumstances. I don't change God's Word to suit my circumstances or to make it comfortable to the flesh. Rather, I change myself and my circumstances by the Word of God to suit Him. I have to line up with God's Word. Jesus is my Provider."

So resist the spirit of poverty from entering your life. Get rid of "stinking thinking" concerning God's blessings. Determine within yourself that even though others have gone into excess in this area, you won't. Determine that you are going to walk in the blessings of God. If you take these truths and become single-minded about them, you will receive God's blessings.

3

REAPING ALWAYS FOLLOWS SOWING

Cast your bread upon the waters, for you will find it after many days. In the morning sow your seed, and in the evening withhold not your hands, for you know not which shall prosper, whether this or that, or whether both alike will be good.

Ecclesiastes 11:1,6 (Amplified)

This passage of Scripture talks about sowing and planting seed. It's interesting to note that today, in certain circles, money is called "bread." Have you heard that expression, "Hey, Joe, did you bring the bread?" I want you to realize that the very thing that will stop you and hinder you from sowing is what will stop you and hinder you from reaping.

If you are waiting for every condition to be favorable, you'll never sow — and you'll never reap. Some people have come to us and said, "Brother Rodney, one day, when everything's just wonderful, we're going to get behind your ministry and support it." We have been waiting for years. Every time I see them, I ask, "How are you doing?" Their response is , "Ah, brother, we're just waiting. We have a big oil deal coming through."

Instead of just doing things systematically and working the small "stuff," these people are always waiting for some big deal. It's usually an astronomical figure like forty million dollars "that is just going to come through." Every time you talk to them, they say, "It'll be another month, but it'll come through. Things are hung up somewhere in Switzerland. It's going through government channels and it's hung up."

Well, I have found out that it isn't the millionaires who finance the Gospel. It's the little widow woman with the two mites, the little bit of oil and the little bit of meal. They are the people who support the Gospel.

Seedtime and Harvest

The Bible talks about seed time and harvest. When you sow, you're planting a seed. If you have children, you know that the many hours you spend every day with them are a seed you are planting into their lives. And you expect to see a return in the years to come.

A good farmer who plows up a field and plants seed is going to wait for the harvest. You don't go to a farmer and tell him, "Look, I know you're planting a field here, but don't really expect a harvest." He's going to look at you and say, "What do you mean. That's why I am here. I'm planting so that I can reap a harvest." Don't let some religious dingbats tell you that you are meant to give, but you really shouldn't expect to receive anything in return.

Some people only reap every month because they only sow every month. Others reap once a year because they only sow once a year. When I read Ecclesiastes 11:6, **In the morning sow your seed, and in the evening do not withhold your hand**....I realize He isn't talking about once-a-week giving or once-a-month giving. I realize God is talking about being a giver — sowing morning and night, and in fact, every waking moment. We must continuously ask ourselves, "How can I be a blessing? How can I do something to help others?"

Faithful With Little, Faithful With Much

So when people come along and say, "Look, if we get a million dollars, we'll give it to you." You need to remind them that if they can't give the five dollars they have in their pocket right now, why should God ever give them a million?

The story of the two boys that grew up together in the same town is a great example. One went to Bible school and studied to become a missionary. The other went to an agricultural school and later on became a successful farmer.

The young man, just as he was about to go out on the mission field, went back to his home town and was ministering at the church. His friend came up to him and said, "I'm so happy to see you. You know, we both chose different courses. You are going on the mission field and I am a successful farmer. I want you to know that I think it's wonderful that you are obeying the call of God. You know, if I had two cars, I would give you one. In fact, if I had two houses, I would give you one. Even if I had two million dollars, I would give one million dollars to you." The missionary replied, "That's wonderful! Tell me, if you had two pigs, would you give one to me?" The farmer answered, "Now, that's not fair. You know I have two pigs."

Giving was fine as long as it related to something that was fictitious — something that was symbolic. God doesn't want what you don't have. It's not the amount you give anyway. It's the attitude of your heart when you give. If you give with the right attitude, God will see that you reap the blessings because He looks upon the heart.

When the offering bucket comes by, you are putting into it what represents your time, your effort, your sweat and your entire life. If you never sow, you will never reap. It doesn't matter who you are. You can fast all day, you can quote Scripture all day, you can pray all day, but if you don't get off your blessed assurance and start sowing and mixing faith with the seed that you've sown, you will never reap.

Become a Giver In Every Area of Your Life

The Bible says, **The generous soul will be made rich, and he who waters will also be watered himself** (Prov. 11:25). Show me somebody who is a giver and I'll show you somebody who is a reaper. Show me somebody who's a stingy tight-wad and I will show you somebody who's always in lack.

Even so, some people are not in lack because they're stingy. They lack because they simply spend too much money. If your outgo exceeds your income, then your upkeep is going to be your downfall. People come to me and say, "Brother Rodney, the devil is attacking my finances." If you are that kind of spender, the devil doesn't need to attack you. You are doing it yourself. It's you who wrote that check, or your wife who has the credit cards. Don't blame the devil.

If this is your problem, ask God to give you wisdom. Then, you won't spend money you don't have to buy things to please people you don't even like. You won't end up with things you never use. Have you ever tuned in the television channel and been told what you need. Have you ever bought from the home shopping club? It's amazing how people seem to find money to get the things they want. If they desperately want it, they find the money to get it. I always make religious devils mad when I talk along this subject of giving. It doesn't take long, as the truth is presented, they hit the door.

Purpose in your heart to become a giver in every area of your life. As you plant in the morning and in the evening, God's blessings will overtake you.

4

GOD IS IN THE MULTIPLICATION BUSINESS

And beware lest you say in your (mind and) heart, My power and the might of my hand have gotten me this wealth. But you shall (earnestly) remember the Lord your God, for it is He Who gives you power to get wealth, that He may establish His covenant which He swore to your fathers, as it is this day.

Deuteronomy 8:17,18 (Amplified)

If you ever hear a self-made person talk about his life, he would say something like, "When I was 21 years old I did this... and when I was 26 years old I did that ...and when I was 30 years old I was at the top...and look at me now. I am a self-made man. I did it my way. I listened to Frank Sinatra every day and did it my way."

The Scripture, however, says,

Some trust in chariots, and some in horses; But we will remember the name of the Lord our God.

Psalm 20:7

Command those who are rich in this present age not to be haughty, nor to trust in uncertain riches but in the living God, who gives us richly all things to enjoy.

1 Timothy 6:17

The Bible says that *...the love of money is a root of all kinds of evil...* (1 Tim. 6:10). Money is not the root of evil — the *love* of money is. The Bible also says that **...God, for it is He who gives you power to get wealth...** (Deut. 8:18). This statement seems to be contrary to what many churches preach. Why? Because God wants to anoint you to acquire wealth in order to establish His covenant. If you have read these principles in the Bible, you need to live them and put them into practice.

Hearers and Doers of the Word

You may know that God wants to save you. You may know that God wants to heal you. And you may know that God wants to prosper you. But are you living this knowledge? Just knowing the Word isn't going to cause it to work in your life. It's acting upon the Word of God and appropriating His promises on a daily basis that does.

Remember the devil also knows the Word. He is a legalist concerning the misquoted Word. When he came to Eve, he said, "Did God say?" When he came to Jesus, he said, "If thou be the Son of God...for it is written." He likes to put people in bondage with Scripture quoted out of context. He even quoted Scripture against Jesus. But Jesus came right back with a Scripture, quoted correctly, which cancelled out his attack. There is a difference between *knowing* the truth and *acting* on it.

When we travel throughout the country, we can actually walk in a church and sense the spirit of poverty that hangs over the people. It's a spirit of fear. It's as if the people live in fear of not making it. They walk in fear of the times they are living in. If you think these are hard times, let's take you on a world tour for a while. Let's go visit some third world countries and you will come back here and thank God for what you have.

Did you know that there are about 380 million motor cars in the world and 160 million are here in America? What does that leave the rest of the four billion people? I hear people talk about how bad times are. But in reality we are extremely blessed. Thank God for America. Thank God for what you have today. There are people half of the world away who are going to bed hungry. You are blessed. The Bible says God gives you the power — or you could say the anointing or the ability — to get wealth so that the Gospel can be preached. The only thing you can take with you when you leave this earth is people. MasterCard, Visa and American "Distress" don't work when you leave earth.

So everybody talks today about investing. "Do you have something for your retirement? Do you have stock, shares or some investment?" But there is something beyond retirement. There is a life after death. Yes, your money can help you here, but what on earth are you doing for heaven's sake? The question is, What are *you* — not your brother — doing for the kingdom of God with what He has given you?

The Parable of the Talents

The Bible tells us in Matthew 25:14-30 the Parable of the Talents ... there was one talent... and three talents... and five talents. The servant with one talent went and buried it, and God called him a slothful servant. The servant with five went and worked hard and ended up with his own increase plus what the servant with one had. God took the one away from the servant with one talent and gave it to the servant with five.

Some people want to redistribute the wealth of the world. But even if they did, within a short period of time it would all come back in the hands of a few people. Why? Because they are wise. Even the Bible says that the children of the world are wiser in the affairs of money than the children of light. (Luke 16:8.)

Some people get saved and then lose their brains. They eat too much pizza, have some revelation and get involved in some "deal." They lose their common sense. Do you know why the message of prosperity has been attacked? Because people went over into excess and were looking for some get-rich-quick scheme. There is no such thing, and if there is, it's probably illegal, immoral or fattening!

The Bible says that the hand of the diligent will lead to plenty. (Prov. 10:4.) There are people in the world who don't have anything else to look for. They work morning, noon and night. They are faithful to their job. They have really nothing to live for, but to work and come into great riches.

Christians get saved and then sit at home. If you ask them what they are doing, they usually say, "Well, I'm sitting here, waiting for God. He's going to give me a deal." No, He is not. You better get off your blessed assurance and start working.

People come crying, "Brother Rodney, I got hired to be a secretary and I got fired." Why? "Because I was reading my Bible." Well, were you hired to read your Bible, or were you hired to type? People wonder why they're not blessed, but they never put in a full day's work. It seems as if everybody wants a handout. People need to learn to take responsibility for themselves. Don't feel sorry for yourself and think that you have been treated wrongly.

Be a Blessing to Others

A long time ago I made a decision that I was not going to be the one walking around with a bucket asking people to "gimme, gimme" me. Instead, I decided to be the one with the bucket dishing money out. I said to myself, "Bless God, I know the Word of God can work for me because I know His Word is true and He doesn't lie."

God's in the multiplication business. He knows how to take a little and make it much. He took a little boy's lunch and fed a multitude. One theologian said, "That wasn't such a miracle. They were big loaves." He had studied it out. "There were large loaves in those days." Can you imagine the little boy's mother saying, "Where are you going with five huge loaves and a whale?" "I am going to lunch, mom." No, it *was* a little boy's lunch.

Some people seem to look at others and think, "Well, they're better off than we are." If anybody's being blessed of God, then people get jealous instead of using their life as an example to say, "*I* can do it, *I* can run on." They get offended instead of getting inspired to receive what God has already given them. These people chose to go around with the poverty mentality that has been passed on to them from generation to generation.

This is particularly true of people whose families lived during the Great Depression. They were told, "When I was in school, we walked barefoot through six feet of snow and we enjoyed it. We didn't have clothes; instead, we had sacks that were sown together and we were happy to have them."

We have to change our entire way of thinking. The only way our thinking can change is by the Word of God. Some people have plain, stinking thinking, especially when it comes to money. If you are one of those people who say, "God doesn't want us to have anything," I can only tell you, "How selfish can you be? How can you be a blessing if you don't have anything?"

God's in the multiplication business. To some, He will give creative ideas and business propositions. If you are a lady staying at home and raising your children, God will inspire you to do something at home that will bring in extra income. And, if you purpose in your heart and say, "God, show me how to bring in more finances to further the Gospel," you will be absolutely amazed at what God will do. In the end, you will give nine-tenths and keep one-tenth for yourself because your blessings will be so abundant.

WHERE ARE YOU PUTTING YOUR TREASURE?

Do not gather and heap up and store up for yourselves treasures on earth, where moth and rust and worm consume and destroy, and where thieves break through and steal.

But gather and heap up and store up for yourselves treasures in heaven, where neither moth nor rust nor worm consume and destroy, and where thieves do not break through and steal; For where your treasure is, there will your heart be also.

Matthew 6:19-21 (Amplified)

It is clear from these Scriptures that there is a place of storage in heaven. Of course, there is also a place of storage on earth. I believe that God wants people to be blessed with heaven's best down here on earth. But it is more important to lay up treasure in heaven. So when we put all our effort and energy into spreading the Gospel, you get blessed by God.

The Bible says, **The blessings of the Lord, it maketh rich, and he addeth no sorrow with it** (Prov. 10:22 KJV). Everything in our ministry has come by the blessing of the

Lord and by the prompting of the Lord. God made the way. He gave us supernatural, divine favor and we have been able to get things in the natural at heavenly prices. We never pay the price that is on the sticker for anything we buy.

Our Faith Is In God, Not In Man

God doesn't mind if you have a nice home, a nice car and all your needs met. However, He is concerned if your heart is in those things. What would happen if those things are taken from you? Would you be totally devastated?

In our lives, we have developed an attitude about everything we own. We can just give them all away today and it wouldn't really bother us. If everything were to be taken away from me today, I would just take my wife and my kids and go. Within eighteen months, somewhere else, we would be blessed again, because our faith is not based on the things that we have or don't have. Our faith is based on the Almighty God.

We are not depending upon material things as our source. We are not even depending solely upon giving. If no one gives to our ministry, we are still going to make it. You may ask, "How is this possible?" Because our faith is not in men, our faith is in God.

When your treasure is on earthly things, you are in trouble. When your treasure is in heaven, you are always going to come out victorious. So, don't get to the other side and find out you had nothing laid up.

You Must Pay the Price

Today, many ministers expect that they can just walk into a ministry and everything will just be handed to them on a platter. People don't seem to be prepared to pay the price tag — work is the price of success in the ministry. I tell evangelists who are going on the field, "Don't expect first-class tickets and five-star hotels everywhere." Whether you are in the ministry or not, you can't just expect to step into someone else's place. You have to work your way into the things of God, appropriate His promises and then, you will begin to see His blessings. What God's done for one, He will do for others.

You have to act upon the Word of God. The only way I know to do that in relationship to your finances is to be a giver. I'm not just talking about offerings. I'm talking about giving in every area of your life — be a giver, sow, give of yourself daily.

Instead of going around looking for somebody to give to you, go around looking to be a blessing to others. Don't be like the world, don't expect something for nothing. It doesn't come that way. You are living in a make-believe world if you think this is how the blessings will come.

Remember, there are two places to store up treasures — heaven and earth. The place where you store your treasures doesn't go unnoticed by God. The Bible says, **For God is not unrighteous to forget your work and labour of love, which ye have shewed toward his name, in that ye have ministered to the saints, and do minister** (Heb. 6:10 KJV). God looks at the little things.

In Luke 6:38, the Lord says:

Give, and it shall be given to you; good measure, pressed down, shaken together, and running over, shall men give into your bosom. For with the same measure that you mete withal it shall be measured to you again (KJV).

On the other hand, the world says exactly the contrary, "Keep hold of what you have because you are going to need it."

Heaven's bank is not based on some savings and loan institution. It's not linked to the world's economy. Aren't you excited about that? In heaven's bank account, you can have more than one hundred thousand dollars. You don't need FDIC insurance.

No One Can Serve Two Masters

One of the biggest problems that people who go into the ministry have is that they want to live in the same living standards as when they were in the business world. They want to step into the ministry and look the same way as they did before, but they are not prepared to pay the price.

When you come into the things of God, you start at the bottom of the ladder and you begin all over again. He will make the way where there is no way. But you have to put your trust in Him and not in your things. You cannot serve God and mammon at the same time.

Because God knows the heart of man, He exhorts us through the Word to not be anxious, uneasy or worried about our life. (Matt. 6:25-33.) God doesn't want you to be worried about what you are going to eat or drink. He wants us to believe that He knows what we need and that He will provide. If God can look after the birds and the flowers, isn't He going to look after you? When this truth starts burning in your heart, God can bless you with all kinds of things. Then you will have the realization in your spirit that no matter what happens, God will take care of you.

Expect God's Best

When this realization becomes a part of you, you will be like a "Holy Ghost Rambo." You will be able to survive even if you have nothing. No matter where you are in the world, the Word of God will work for you. You will be blessed and the hand of God will bring you forth. You will walk through life with the favor of God. That's why I always expect God's best at heavenly prices.

It's not a game so that you can go around and just freeload on everybody. It's so that you can be a blessing. And don't think that it works for me just because I'm in the ministry. It will work for you too.

God knows what your needs are. But He says, "Seek me, make the Kingdom of God and His righteousness a priority in your life. Then all these things will be given to you." What a wonderful promise! Therefore, don't worry about tomorrow because God will give you the victory and the joy you need for each day.

Transfer Your Riches to Heaven

We have to transfer our riches from the earth below to heaven above. I'm not telling you to give away your house and your car and everything you have. Just keep in mind that your home is not here. Everything you use on the earth is just a means to an end. You are just a steward of what God has given you while you are on earth. These are temporary, residing quarters.

Let your prayer be, "I do not live for myself, I live for others. My treasure is not on the earth." Constantly remind yourself that your treasure is not on the earth, it is in heaven. You're just passing through. You are on your way to a fairer land. I pray that the Holy Spirit will stir up your heart today so that you may have the revelation of this truth.

STEWARDSHIP BASED ON GOD'S WORD, NOT GIMMICKS

We want to tell you further, brethren, about the grace (the favor and the spiritual blessing) of God which has been evident in the churches of Macedonia (arousing in them the desire to give alms).

2 Corinthians 8:1 (Amplified)

The Scripture says that the favor and the spiritual blessing of God was evident in the churches of Macedonia. So much so that it aroused in them the desire to give alms. Whenever God's blessing is evident and His power is being displayed, people desire to give. On the other hand, when the anointing is not present, some ministries try to resort to gimmicks to manipulate people into giving.

Have you seen the television program where you are told, "I'll send you a shower cap with the hand of blessing in it. When you put on, there shall be showers of blessing." Or, "We will send you a piece of the old rugged cross and you will receive the blessings." Have you ever received their partner appeal letters that say, "Neighbor, as I was praying for you today..." But they don't even know you. You are just a name that came out of the computer. Do you know the gimmicks coming from the Church are the brainchild of fund-raising agencies and money grabbing people who make merchandise out of God's servants?

Many ministers got hooked up in this trap, but the days of the abuse of mailing lists are over. God's people are either going to be taught how to give through the Word of God or not give at all. If you are only giving because I have mail coming to you every two weeks and you can stick my face on your fridge, stop giving. If that's the only reason you give, you are giving for the wrong reason and you are never going to see the blessing of God come in your life.

Spirit-Led Giving

You must give because the Word of God and the Spirit of God tell you to give. Spirit-led giving will produce results in your life. You are not to give just because you see a need. You are to give because you are led of God. A person who is truly led by the Holy Spirit will not always go around and let you know what their needs are. The Bible says, let your requests be made known unto God. (Phil. 4:6,7.)

When I teach in Africa, the African people are amazed at how many people give to my ministry. Somebody told me, "Oh, you know the people in the United Kingdom don't give." I said, "They will if I go there." They asked, "How can you be sure that people will give?" My answer was, "Because I'm going to teach on giving." This was also the case when I went to Australia. They told me that they had never given any evangelist the amount of money they gave me. They said, "Where did it come from? You never begged, you just taught on giving." When people are taught the Word of God, they want to obey the Word of God. That is God's way. He doesn't want us to put pressure on anybody. People who give to my ministry are never pressured to give.

Whenever the anointing of God is present, people want to give — they want to be a part of what God is doing. But, the moment the anointing leaves, then there is a need to talk about all the bad news, "Well, a tornado hit our mission in Africa and blew the roof off. We need $10,000 this week." The next time you tune in, "This morning there was a hurricane in Tahiti." The next day is an earthquake in Nicaragua. It seems as if some ministries have a different crisis every day, especially the guys on television. You want to ask them, "What disaster are you in today?" They want me to do as they say, but I wonder why. They seem to be in worse shape than I am. Then they tell me I need a miracle and that if I want to receive my miracle, I must give to give them "their miracle." Those are all the wrong reasons to give.

Don't Give to Man, Give to God

You should invest into the Gospel. But in the western world, especially in America, everybody has been geared into brick and mortar. They found out that people in the west would rather give to a building than to the lost because they wanted something tangible in exchange for their giving. This is also the wrong motive. That's why people who give in this fashion cannot be blessed.

When you put your finances in the offering, you release them into the Kingdom of God. They do not die in the bucket. You are not giving to man. You are giving directly to God. If that person abuses that which you have given, God will deal with him. And if you, as a minister of the Gospel, abuse that which God gives you, the first thing that will go is the anointing.

Giving With Abundance of Joy

For in the midst of an ordeal of severe tribulation, their abundance of joy and their depth of poverty (together) have overflowed in wealth of lavish generosity on their part.

For, as I can bear witness, (they gave) according to their ability, yes, and beyond their ability; and (they did it) voluntarily.

2 Corinthians 8:2,3 (Amplified)

The Church in Macedonia was in the midst of great trial of affliction. They were living under conditions of severe tribulation. Today in America people think they are living in severe tribulation because gas went up two cents a gallon. As long as you can get a hamburger for forty-nine cents, you are not living in severe tribulation. When you have to stand in bread lines for four hours, then you can say, "I think this is severe tribulation."

Despite their condition, the Church in Macedonia was in abundance of joy. How can you have abundance of joy in the midst of tribulation? Because joy and happiness are two different things. Happiness is based on circumstances. Some people have never learned to live with the joy of the Lord bubbling out of their belly. Their happiness is attached to their circumstances. If everything is up, they are up. If everything is down, they are down. They are like a puppet on a string manipulated by the circumstances of life. But you can have joy in the midst of adverse circumstances.

They gave out of their own free will. The Church in Macedonia did not need to be manipulated in order to give. Ministers today need to realize that they are here for the benefit of those they minister to and that the blessings of God will manifest if they serve the Body of Christ.

I want to exhort you in your giving. Mix faith with it and always be reminded to give for the right reason.

YOU CAN DEPEND ON THE GOOD SHEPHERD

The Lord is my shepherd; I shall not want. He makes me to lie down in green pastures; He leads me beside the still waters. He restores my soul; He leads me in the paths of righteousness for His name's sake.

Yea, though I walk through the valley of the shadow of death, I will fear no evil; For You are with me; Your rod and Your staff, they comfort me. You prepare a table before me in the presence of my enemies; You anoint my head with oil; My cup runs over.

Surely goodness and mercy shall follow me All the days of my life; And I will dwell in the house of the Lord Forever.

Psalm 23

This Psalm give us a picture of the Lord Jesus Christ. Many people have it on their T-shirts or on little magnets that are stuck on their refrigerator or the wall, but they really don't believe it.

Verse 1 says, **The Lord is my shepherd; I shall not want**. Yet, many believe, "The Lord is my shepherd, I am full of wants."

Psalm 23 is a portrayal of the Good Shepherd. I come from Africa and in the southern region of Africa and in Australia there is a lot of sheep farming.

I spent ten years of my life growing up in an African independent country within our borders of the Southern African region called the Transkei. It's on the east coast and borders right on the sea route. This is some of the finest grazing land in the nation. It is a beautiful area with abundant rain. Everybody has sheep in that region and everywhere you go, there are sheep. You have to be careful as you drive along the roads because when one sheep runs, all of them follow. Many cars have hit sheep unexpectedly.

The Hireling Shepherd

Many of the tribal black people in these areas live in a group of several houses surrounded by a wall called a "kraal". Sometimes the men have up to ten wives — sometimes even more. The more powerful they are, the more wives they have. The wives do the work. The men sit on the front porch and smoke a pipe, while the wives go out in the field to work everyday.

With ten wives, these shepherds also have many little children. They have a lot of little boys who really don't help much. They also need many daughters because for each daughter they have and give in marriage, they can get up to one hundred head of cattle. This is called paying *labola*. So if the shepherd has ten daughters, you can imagine how wealthy he will be after a couple of years. The little boys don't have much to do, so they are put in charge of the sheep. It's not uncommon to see a little tiny guy of only five or six years of age running around and being the shepherd of about a hundred sheep.

The little boy is not with the sheep constantly. When the night comes or when he is hungry, he goes home. If a hyena or an animal tries to attack the sheep, he's not going to defend them — he's gone and the sheep are left to the devourer.

The True Shepherd

If you go to the middle east, however, you see a different portrayal of a shepherd. He comes from a line of shepherds. He lives with the sheep. He smells like the sheep and, maybe, even starts looking like the sheep after a while. They are just a different breed. They are with the sheep constantly. He's there if the wolf, the lion or the bear come. As a shepherd boy, David took the lion and the bear. He was there to defend the sheep even with his life if it were necessary.

These are the portrayals of two different types of shepherds — the true shepherd and the hireling one.

The hireling shepherd can't be blamed. He may be only five years of age and if trouble comes, he's gone. The sheep don't really know him because he hasn't been around that long. So when he talks, they never listen to him. If he gets up and walks ahead, they never follow him because they don't know him.

The true shepherd, as you can see them in the middle east, will sit down or lean against a rock. He'll get up, take his staff and start to walk. All he might need to say is, "Come on," and they will start to follow him. There is a lot of work that goes into being a true shepherd. For example, sheep can't drink from a fast running brook. If they try, the water flows over their noses and they could drown. So the shepherd cuts a U-shape area into the bank and allows an area of still water to form so that the sheep can drink safely. If the shepherd loses one sheep, he leaves the ninety-nine and goes off to the one. A true shepherd will defend his sheep with his life.

Jesus Is Our Good Shepherd

When I read Psalm 23, I see a beautiful portrayal of the Lord Jesus Christ as the True Shepherd and I am reminded of what Jesus said, **My sheep hear my voice... The voice of a stranger, they will not follow.**(John 10:4,5,27.)

The hireling shepherd has to use whips or dogs to drive the sheep. But Jesus never drives anybody — He doesn't force anyone. That's the difference between Christianity and a cult. Cults are always forcing people. Some denominations and groups, even Pentecostal Charismatic, border on cult-like practices in the way they manipulate and control people — sometimes through intimidation. Jesus never does that. He leads us. It's our choice whether we follow Him or not.

I encourage you to see Jesus as the Good Shepherd. If He came to your house today, He would not bring up any past sins or condemn you. He would only look at you with loving eyes. When Peter denied the Lord on three different occasions, Jesus never said to him, "Peter, you let me down. You failed me very badly and you let me down in the darkest hour of my life. I'll never trust you again."

Instead, Jesus just looked at Him with loving eyes and said, **...Simon, son of Jonah, do you love me more than these?** That must have melted everything within Peter.

He said to Him, Yes, Lord, You know that I love You. He said to him, feed My lambs. He said to him a second time, Simon, son of Jonah, do you love Me? He said to Him, Yes, Lord; You know that I love You. He said to him, Tend My sheep. He said to him the third time, Simon son of Jonah, do you love me? Peter was grieved because He said to him the third time, Do you love Me? And he said to Him, Lord, You know all things; you know that I love You. Jesus said to him, Feed My sheep.

John 21:15,16

Isn't it amazing that Peter denied the Lord three times and here Jesus took him back through three affirmations of Peter's love for Him. Jesus reinstated Peter and brought him back into a place of fellowship and then confirmed to him his calling and ministry.

Feed the Flock of God

Our job, as ministers of the Lord Jesus Christ, whether we are in the five-fold ministry or in the ministry of reconciliation (every believer has that responsibility), is to feed the flock of God — to take care of the sheep of God.

You are not here for my benefit, but rather, I am here for your benefit. I'm here to serve you. You are not here to serve me. The last thing that Jesus did before He left the earth was to wash His disciples feet — He served them.

The Lord is my Shepherd (to feed, guide, and shield me), I shall not lack.

Psalm 23:1 (Amplified)

You need to have the divine revelation of Psalm 23 in your life. The Good Shepherd has made provision for all your needs. Learn to trust in Him today.

GIVING WITH THE RIGHT ATTITUDE

That is why I thought it necessary to urge these brethren to go to you before I do and make arrangements in advance for this bountiful, promised gift of yours, so that it may be ready, not as an extortion (wrung out of you) but as a generous and willing gift. (Remember) this: he who sows sparingly and grudgingly will also reap sparingly and grudgingly, and he who sows generously (that blessings may come to someone) will also reap generously and with blessings.

Let each one (give) as he has made up his own mind and purposed in his heart, not reluctantly or sorrowfully or under compulsion, for God loves (He takes pleasure in, prizes above other things, and is unwilling to abandon or to do without) a cheerful (joyous, "prompt to do it") giver (whose heart is in his giving). And God is able to make all grace (very favor and earthly blessing) come to you in abundance, so that you may always and under all circumstances and whatever the need be self-sufficient (possessing enough to require no aid or support and furnished in abundance for every good work and charitable donation).

2 Corinthians 9:5-8 (Amplified)

A person who has a heart full of deceit regarding money will also have a heart of deceit regarding the anointing. In God's economy the people who have more, get more. I know that doesn't make sense in the world we live in today.

In some countries, the government wants to redistribute the wealth and make the poor wealthy. But if they did that, in a short period of time, the rich would be poor again. Because wealth and poverty are just the symptoms of a deeper root which is the attitude of the heart of man.

Did you know that there's enough money in the world to make everybody on the planet a millionaire? But even if this happened, tomorrow there would be some who would lose it and others who would keep it. I believe that God wants to exhort us in the area of our giving and finances because of the harvest that must be reaped in these last days.

Can God Entrust His Wealth to You?

Proverbs 13:22 says, **The wealth of the sinner is stored up for the righteous.** The bottom line is, God cannot really entrust the wealth of the sinner to the just at this time. I don't want to offend anybody, but that's just the truth. God cannot really entrust the wealth of the sinner to the Church because the Church doesn't even know what to do with what they have now. What would they do if they had the wealth of the world?

The Church has been erecting many buildings that end up as white elephants. The Body of Christ is lined with giant Ishmaels that will forever speak of man's ability to dream and create. But there's a harvest to be reaped.

(Remember) this: he who sows sparingly and grudgingly will also reap sparingly and grudgingly, and he who sows generously (that blessings may come to someone) will also reap generously and with blessings.

God doesn't want an offering that is received under pressure. He desires for His people to purpose in their heart to give back to God for the work of the ministry — **not grudgingly or of necessity.** I find that there are some preachers who are nothing more than extortionists. They wring the money out of the people.

God looks at the heart of people. God doesn't want to force you or coerce you to tithe. It is part of our Christian life to give. It is important that we understand the difference between Bible giving and manipulation. God wants a generous, willing gift from a cheerful giver.

Are You Happy With Your Harvest?

You say, "Brother Rodney, I'm not happy with what I'm reaping." Check out what you are sowing. You say, "Brother Rodney, I have people give things to me, but they don't give with the right attitude." Maybe it is time to check your own attitude towards giving.

I knew of a church who took a missionary offering. Do you know what was in it? Used tea bags for the missionaries. Some people say, "I have an old car with 150,000 miles on it. It's falling to pieces and the tires are bald. We want to send it to the mission field." About the only thing that this car can be used for is a chicken coop. Why send them some old piece of junk, so it can break down in the bush and become a place for chickens? Someone asks, "Where is the vehicle we sent you last year?" The answer is, "Oh, yes, we drove 1000 miles and now it has chickens in it. It's getting ten chickens a gallon."

Give Generously

But when you give, give generously so you can reap the blessings. Once, I asked a man, "Why do you raise your hands to the offering?" He said, "I'm waving my money good-bye!"

Don't give sorrowfully or under compulsion just because you feel compelled to give. Don't give just because someone says, "If you don't give, we are going off the air." When God calls you to an area of ministry, He will pay for it. He will equip you to get the job done, and if you keep going in the hole, something is wrong.

I tell preachers that if the anointing is present, the needs are met and you know you're in the right place. But when the well dries up and there is no anointing, don't resort to some gimmick. Get back to your call. Get back to what God tells you to do and He will meet your needs.

Sufficiency in All Things

God's plan for our finances and the ministry is laid out in 2 Corinthians 9:8:

And God is able to make all grace (very favor and earthly blessing) come to you in abundance, so that you may always and under all circumstances and whatever the need be self-sufficient (possessing enough to require no aid or support and furnished in abundance for every good work and charitable donation).

Therefore be encouraged and remember that the attitude with which you give is what God sees. If you're just pulling money out of your wallet, or writing out a check and just throwing it in the bucket without mixing faith, *stop!* You need to ponder a little bit about what you are doing and remember that you need to worship God with your giving.

You need to give on the basis of the Word of God alone. We need to give because we want to be givers. I give because God is a giver. I give because He gave me Jesus. I give because Jesus has given me everything I have. So, I look for things to give. It doesn't have to stop with the offering. We can give much more than money.

When you see someone who is prospering, don't get jealous. Find out what they're doing! When I see other people blessed, I rejoice. I let them be a beacon on the sea. I let their faith spur me on and encourage me. Then, I think, "Lord, if You can do it for him, if You can bless him, he must be doing something right. I'm going to find out what he is doing."

Ask God what He would have you do and then you just obey the Holy Spirit as He guides you. If you obey Him, you are going to get blessed. Don't be trapped by the pressure used by some who manipulate the Body of Christ. Don't allow gimmicks to force you into giving, "We are going to take the Isaiah 41:10 offering now. Everybody give $41.10." These are gimmicks. Your giving must be directed by the Holy Spirit. If you feel any pressure to give, just wave the bucket good-bye when it passes you.

Give with a heart filled with gladness and believe that for every dollar you sow, there will be a soul saved, a life touched, a church revived here in America. Make sure that you are giving with the attitude that agrees with 2 Corinthians 9:5-8 and you will be greatly blessed!

WORSHIP THE LORD AND GIVE WITH A THANKFUL HEART

Now concerning the collection for the saints, as I have given orders to the churches of Galatia, so you must do also: On the first day of the week let each one of you lay something aside, storing up as he may prosper, that there be no collections when I come.

And when I come, whomever you approve by your letters I will send to bear your gift to Jerusalem. But if it is fitting that I go also, they will go with me.

1 Corinthians 16:1-4

The Apostle Paul is encouraging them to give as they have been blessed — as they have prospered — and to put something aside. The Bible tells us in Malachi 3:10:

"Bring all the tithes into the storehouse, that there may be food in My house, and try Me now in this," says the Lord of hosts, "If I will not open for you the windows of heaven and pour out for you such blessing that there will not be room enough to receive it."

This wonderful promise has to be present in our mind and our spirit when we give. We cannot give out of tradition. "Let's get the offering boxes out, let's get the buckets out. It's time to give." People reach for their wallets and put an amount in. They never even think or pray about it. Some have never even sat down and counted their blessings.

Count Your Blessings

Do you know that old song that says, "Count your blessings, name them one by one." Unfortunately, we know of some circles that have actually mocked this message. But when you sit down and you count your blessings, you start to name them one by one. And something happens. You will be surprised at what the Lord has done. It's so easy to forget. It's so easy to think, "I am just having such a hard time and things aren't going that well." It is so easy to start looking at little things and missing out on what God is doing.

We ought to be mindful of the blessing of God which we receive on a daily basis. We ought to be mindful that His hand is upon us and that if it weren't for the Lord and His grace, who knows where we would be. Sometimes it's so easy to forget His benefits to us.

Worship God For His Abundant Supply

When we look back and recall the abundant blessings that God has bestowed upon us, our hearts are filled with thanksgiving. Therefore, when you have the opportunity to come into the house of the Lord to bring your tithes and offerings, remember to worship God. We worship Him with our increase, with a small portion of all that which He has entrusted to us.

I have made a conscious decision to sow my tithes and offerings into the ministry, expecting that my investment will carry out the plan and purpose of God. Worship God with your giving. Not just as some action that is done in the spur of the moment. Don't just give something because it is time to take the offering.

There are a lot of people who want the blessing of God, but they don't want to do anything for it. They are spiritual free-loaders. They always go around expecting something for nothing. That's why all the scams here in America survive, because there are so many greedy people wanting something for nothing. When they come to the kingdom of God, they once again want something for nothing and this contradicts Scripture. As God has prospered you, give. As God has blessed you, give.

Purpose in Your Heart To Honor the Lord

Husbands and wives get together and purpose in your heart to worship God with your tithing. The tithe doesn't go all over the place. It comes to the storehouse where you get fed the Word of God. If you like the food, put your money where your mouth is. God sees your heart and the attitude with which you give. Sometimes people forget. They think it is just an offering, "Quickly, lets get it out of the way." No. It is time that we worship God with our giving. It's time to honor God with our finances.

By faithfully bringing your tithe every Sunday, every payday, every chance you get, you are saying, "God, I present to You one tenth of that which You have given to me so that we can win more souls into Your kingdom. I fully expect Your blessings to be unfolded in every area of my life. Today, I am expecting God's blessing to rain down upon me."

If you have not been worshipping the Lord by tithing and giving offerings, purpose in your heart today to start obeying God with a joyful heart — and watch what God will do in your life!

10

THE LAW OF SEEDTIME AND HARVEST

Give to everyone who asks of you. And from him who takes away your goods do not ask them back. And just as you want men to do to you, you also do to them likewise.

But if you love those who love you, what credit is that to you? For even sinners love those who love them. And if you do good to those who do good to you, what credit is that to you? For even sinners do the same.

And if you lend to those from whom you hope to receive back, what credit is that to you? For even sinners lend to sinners to receive as much back. But love your enemies, do good, and lend, hoping for nothing in return; and your reward will be great, and you will be sons of the Most High. For He is kind to the unthankful and evil.

Therefore be merciful, just as your Father also is merciful. Judge not, and you shall not be judged. Condemn not, and you shall not be condemned. Forgive, and you will be forgiven. Give, and it will be given to you: good measure, pressed down, shaken together, and running over will be put into your bosom. For with the same measure that you use, it will be measured back to you.

Luke 6:30-38

The best way to get rid of any resentment you might have towards someone is to give to that person. Send an offering to those who have wronged you. Some big ministers have publicly criticized my ministry. When this happened, I sent them an offering. Later on, they were shown to be wrong.

People ask me, "Why do you give money to that person?" I need to do that to release myself, because you can't give to someone you hate. You have to love them in order to give. When you love a person and you sow to them, something happens in the spiritual realm which releases you and places them in God's hands. And when God gets through with them, their attitude is rearranged.

Leave Them in God's Hands

The Bible says that **vengeance belongs to the Lord and that He will repay** (Deut. 32:35). When you judge other people and take judgment into your hands, you take it out of the hands of God. When you love them and don't render evil for evil, God will deal with them.

The best thing to do, is to give up resentment, let it drop. You have to protect your heart. You can't expect to walk in the anointing of God and harbor unforgiveness against other people. You can't expect to walk in the power of God and be critical and judgmental of others. It hinders the anointing of God in your life. This is the reason many ministries that once had the anointing of God and flowed in signs and wonders, are just sitting by the highway of life. God can't use them anymore because they are so bitter — full of resentment and unforgiveness.

Guard Your Heart and Plant Good Seed

Give, and it will be given to you: good measure, pressed down, shaken together, and running over will be put into your bosom. For with the same measure that you use, it will be measured back to you.

Luke 6:38

This promise can be applied both for the positive and the negative things of life. If you give a good measure of strife, you will get it back — pressed down, shaken together and running over, will strife come back to you. Think about it. What you sow is what you are going to reap.

There's a law on the earth, the law of seedtime and harvest. The seed you plant is going to bring forth a crop. I remember a young couple who came to see me several years ago. They were not married and said, "Brother Rodney, would you pray for us. We've been doing things we shouldn't be doing and now she is pregnant and we want to pray that God will take the baby away." I looked at them and said, "Look, you do the things that make babies, you're going to have babies!" People need to use wisdom. There are laws on the earth. The consequences of these laws come to pass whether we want them to or not. If you sow in the flesh, you are going to reap in the flesh.

The Same Measure You Use, Will Be Measured Back to You

Let's bring this truth to the realm of finances. The Bible says, "Give and it shall be given." When I was a kid, we would go to the candy store. There were containers which you filled with the candy you wanted to buy. Well, I didn't know that they weighed the container. I thought it was one price for as much as you could stuff into the can. So I'd grab the candy and I'd shake it and press it down and pile it high and still ended up paying more. The measure you use to give, sets the measure of what you receive. If you use teaspoonfuls, the measure will come back teaspoonfuls. If you use bucket loads, then you'll be receive back bucket loads in return.

Let's remember that first of all we are worshiping God with our giving. Second, the dollars we give are going into the kingdom of God. Therefore, I am sowing into eternity. I am laying up for myself treasures in heaven. Thirdly, every dollar sown is going to represent a soul that is going to be saved. When you give, you are also releasing your faith for a harvest in the spiritual realm. God is going to bless you in abundance because your seed is going to bring forth a return to you.

Stretch Your Faith

Start believing God for your needs and the needs of those around you. Say, "God, I am going to add my faith to those who are in need. We are going to see a breakthrough in that area." Get involved and help others. As you help them, you are going to help yourself because your are stretching your faith and learning to put your trust in God.

Everybody tries to exercise their faith within the comfort zone, where everything is cut and dried. "I'm working a job, I'm getting a salary every week and I'm living by faith." You are not living by faith. You haven't stretched your faith. Everything is sure. You haven't believed God for anything. You are only in faith when you are so far out there that if God doesn't come to your rescue, you are finished!

When we went in the ministry in 1980, I was learning to believe God. I was believing for the bare necessities. I would hear people say they were believing for ten thousand dollars and I would think, "Lord, have mercy! That's stretching it — not in a hundred years." I would hear of ministries giving other ministries five thousand dollars and I would think, "This is incredible." I thought if I gave fifty dollars I was pushing it — Mr. Giver personified. But something stood up on the inside of me. I said to myself, "If this other minister believes God and is a giver, then the day is coming when I am also going to believe God's Word and become a doer of the Word. I want to be a giver. I want to be able to plant a seed."

I didn't start off with five thousand dollars. God wanted to see if I would be faithful with five dollars. When you are learning to trust God for bigger things, He will instruct you to give to others and you will learn to hear His voice. The Lord may say to you, "Give that person ten dollars."

Will You Obey God?

I was standing in a parking lot talking to a preacher who had just been given a brand new car. He looked like the personification of success. The Lord said to me, "Give him the one-hundred dollar bill you have." I said, "He doesn't need it." And the Lord said, "How do you know he doesn't need it?" I said, "God, somebody just gave him a new car. How can he need a hundred dollars?" I was about to walk away when God started dealing with me. "Give him the hundred dollars." I thought, "No, I am not. He doesn't need it. He is doing well. He just told me how well he is doing." The Lord said again, "Give him the money." Then I knew, there was no point in getting into the car and driving away because I would be so uncomfortable — not worth a hundred dollars.

So I pulled the money out and just slipped it into his hands. The guy started weeping and said, "You wouldn't believe it. I got a new car but I don't have any money to buy gas. This will get me to the next town where I am starting some meetings."

Isn't that amazing? God will test you to see if you are faithful in the small and simple things. I always desired to see the day I could put finances into other ministries. This year alone, our ministry has put close to $400,000 into world missions. I share this to show you that only ten years ago, I didn't think that day would come.

Plant in good soil so that your seed will prosper. I get so excited about the law of seedtime and harvest. Start living in an attitude of giving and watch the release that will come into your own heart. When the things of the earth mean nothing to you, God will entrust to you much, so that you can bless others.

HONOR GOD WITH THE FIRSTFRUITS, NOT THE LEFTOVERS

> Honor the Lord with your possessions, and with the first-fruits of all your increase; so your barns will be filled with plenty, and your vats will overflow with new wine.
>
> Proverbs 3:9,10

I like to focus on honoring God with the firstfruits because I know of people who, at the end of the month, remember that extra money came in and that they need to give one tenth of that income. We need to make the decision to tithe at the moment the money comes in. In other words, it's something we do immediately. The tithe should never be an after-thought.

The Amplified version of the Bible says **to honor the Lord with your capital and sufficiency** (Prov. 3:9). If you tithe as soon as you receive your blessing, you are telling God, "I put You first." This should not only apply to the money that comes in, but to everything else that God gives you — your home, your children, your belongings.

The Truth About Cain and Abel

The Book of Genesis tells the story of Cain and Abel. You could say that Cain was a crop farmer and Abel was a sheep farmer. They both worked the grounds but the products they produced were different. One grew in the ground, the other on top of the ground.

And in the course of time Cain brought to the Lord and offering of the fruit of the ground. And Abel brought of the firstborn of his flock and of the fat portions. And the Lord had respect and regard for Abel and for his offering. But for Cain and his offering He had no respect or regard. So Cain was exceedingly angry and indignant, and he looked sad and depressed.

Genesis 4:3-5 (Amplified)

What are the firstlings? They are the firstfruits. Cain's offering wasn't the firstfruits. He just brought an offering in the process of time.

God had respect for Abel's offering but didn't respect Cain's. Why? Was it because God hated broccoli? Did God get upset because Cain gave him vegetables? Cain's business was not sheep farming. I know everybody says, "God was upset because Cain brought vegetables." No. It had nothing to do with vegetables or sheep. It had to do with "in the course of time" and "firstfruits." God respected and honored Abel's offering above Cain's, because Cain brought his offering in the course of time.

Ananias and Sapphira

The Book of Acts chapter 5 tells us about an offering that was so powerful that two people dropped dead.

But a certain man named Ananias, with Sapphira his wife, sold a possession. And he kept back part of the proceeds, his wife also being aware of it, and brought a certain part and laid it at the apostles' feet. But Peter said, "Ananias, why has Satan filled your heart to lie to the Holy Spirit and keep back part of the price of the land for yourself?

While it remained, was it not your own? And after it was sold, was it not in your own control? Why have you conceived this thing in your heart? You have not lied to men but to God." Then Ananias hearing these words, fell down and breathed his last. So great fear came upon all those who heard these things. And the young men arose and wrapped him up, carried him out, and buried him.

Acts 5:1-6

Now, after an interval of about three hours, Ananias' wife came in. She did not know what had happened and also lied. You could say, "Why did Peter pick on her? One loss in the family is enough. She would have learned her lesson just having lost her husband.

Now it was about three hours later when his wife came in, not knowing what had happened. And Peter answered her, "Tell me whether you sold the land for so much?" And she said, "Yes, for so much." Then Peter said to her, "How is it that you have agreed together to test the Spirit of the Lord? Look, the feet of those who have buried your husband are at the door, and they will carry you out."

Acts 5:7-9

God Looks at the Heart

Why did they die? First of all, they sold the land and said they were going to give the proceeds to God. But then, at the last minute, they reneged and then lied to the Holy Spirit. God really looks upon our hearts when we give. Somebody said, "Are you saying that if I give in the offering or don't give in the offering, I'm going to die?" No. I haven't heard of anybody in recent times dying during the offering. There is a principle that we need to learn.

Abel died over an offering. But he was in the forefront of receiving his brother's anger because his brother's heart was not right. Ananias and Sapphira didn't have to give anything, but they had made a promise that they were not prepared to keep. Instead of telling the truth and giving the part they had agreed to give, they lied and died. They were not obligated to give it *all*. They were only obligated to be truthful concerning the offering that they were prepared to give. What is God trying to tell us? God sees the heart of the giver. No one can fool God. You can say, "Brother Rodney, I just want to give and serve." But God knows exactly what's going on in your heart. We have to realize that an offering is more than just putting some money into the bucket.

God has blessed us with everything we have. We're not doing Him any favors by giving to Him. We are honoring Him. But in reality we are doing ourselves a favor. We need to give, more than God needs to receive from us. He owns everything. He wants to teach us to be good stewards of what He has given us.

Many parents work hard to provide well for their children and would be very hurt if their children responded with ungratefulness or a lack of appreciation.

Likewise, God has done everything to provide for us and when we come to Him with our tithes and offerings, we need to remember we are sowing back into His kingdom. We are saying, "God, my heart is right and I put you first place in my life. Everything I have belongs to you and You can have it all if You want it." But God doesn't want it all, He just wants one tenth. So let's honor Him with our offerings and our firstfruits.

Meditate on what it means to give firstfruits. God always comes first. That's what makes the difference. It shows the "good heart" attitude. The attitude that will bring you the blessing.

Today, we don't have people dropping dead, but we do have people who are deceitful with their finances before God. They are not going to be blessed. Show me a giver and I will show you somebody who is going to be blessed. Show me somebody who is always deceitful in the area of the finances that belong to God, and I'll show you someone who seems to always walk in calamity.

Let me encourage you to honor God with your firstfruits — giving to Him from the top and not off the bottom. Always remember that by giving firstfruits, you honor God and He will fill your household with abundance and your vats will overflow with new wine.

KEEP ON CASTING YOUR BREAD ON THE WATERS

Cast your bread upon the waters, for you will find it after many days. Give a portion to seven, yes, even (divide it) to eight, for you know not what evil may come upon the earth. If the clouds are full of rain, they empty themselves upon the earth; and if a tree falls toward the south or toward the north, in the place where the tree falls, there it will lie. He who observes the wind (and waits for all conditions to be favorable) will not sow, and he who regards the clouds will not reap.

As you know not what is the way of the wind, or how the spirit comes to the bones in the womb of a pregnant woman, even so you know not the work of God, Who does all.

In the morning sow your seed, and in the evening withhold not your hands, for you know not which shall prosper, whether this or that, or whether both alike will be good.

Ecclesiastes 11:1-6 (Amplified)

According to verse 4, focusing on the circumstances usually hinders the blessings of God. People who look at the events of life in the natural, limit themselves and put a ceiling on what

God can do for them. People want to limit God because they are limited.

As Christians, we must remember that those things that seem impossible in our lives are possible with God. He is the God of the impossible. He can make a way where there is none. He can command light to shine out of darkness. He can have water flow from a rock. He can furnish a table in the wilderness.

The Church has tried to limit God by their self-imposed limitations — to put Him in a box, to make Him a man. When it comes to giving, we must look into sowing abundantly in every area of life. You sow friendships, you will reap friendships, you sow love, you will reap love. You sow financially, you'll reap financially.

Sow in the Area of Relationships

People talk about their marriages, "My marriage is not working. I wonder why." Shouting and screaming at each other every day is not going to produce a good marriage. Beating your husband or wife up is not going to help you. People need to be prepared to put one hundred percent into their marriage — not just fifty-fifty. A marriage requires a commitment that gives everything to it.

When you love Jesus, you commit one hundred percent to Him. He has control of every area of your life, including your finances. If He's not Lord *of all*, He is not Lord *at all.* He has to be Lord of every area — your finances, your home, your children, your husband, wife and every decision you make.

It is the little things that we do in life that produce the greatest harvest. In a marriage, it is not so much the once-a-year big splash on the town. It's the small things you do every day — the good-bye kiss when you leave the house in the morning, the one flower that you might bring her or a thoughtful comment.

This principle is also applicable in the relationship you have with your children. It's so important to plant in your children a seed of love. They need to hear every day how much you love them. I do that with my kids all the time. When I have to discipline them, I first tell them that I love them. When they were babies, I used to smother them with kisses. I always cuddled them. Now that they are older, they come running to me in the morning. They so desire to love me. I tell my wife, "I'm reaping for every one of those kisses I've sown."

It's the constant sowing of seed that produces the harvest. The harvest doesn't come from the one-time gift that you sowed. If you cast your bread upon the waters at all times, it's going to come back to you on every wave. (Eccles. 11:1.)

When I was a about six years old, we lived in a coastal town right on the river bank which runs into the Indian Ocean. It was a large river and the tides were very high and would come up to the back wall of the property. So you could just cast a line in and fish. To get me out of the house, my mother used to tell me, "Go out there and wait until my ship comes in." I would sit there, hours going by, waiting for the ship to come in. Well, one day the revelation came to me. There was no ship coming in because she hadn't sent one out. I was waiting for something she had never sent.

If you don't give anything, you are not going to receive anything. The Bible says, **And remember the words of the Lord Jesus, that He said, It is more blessed to give than to receive** (Acts 20:35). This is an attitude that has to be burning deep down in your heart.

When you sow daily in every area of your life, you maintain an attitude of expectancy. You expect the blessings of God so you can bless others on a daily basis. Let your prayer be, "Lord, make me a blessing, allow me to meet other people's needs in every area."

DO YOU QUALIFY FOR PHILIPPIANS 4:19?

And my God will liberally supply (fill to the full) your every need according to His riches in glory in Christ Jesus.

Philippians 4:19 (Amplified)

This is a widely-known Bible Scripture. It has been stuck on magnets that go on the refrigerator. It has been put on bumper stickers, placed on cars so old they have been held together with baling wire. It has been printed on T-shirts. Yet, this Scripture doesn't seem to profit until it is hidden in the heart of the believer.

A lot of people know a Scripture, but they don't know the context in which it was given. If you ask people, "What does Philippians 4:15-18 say? They usually don't know. So, let's find out.

And you Philippians yourselves well know that in the early days of the Gospel ministry, when I left Macedonia, no church (assembly) entered into partnership with me and opened up (a debit and credit) account in giving and receiving except you only.

For even in Thessalonica you sent (me contributions) for my needs, not only once but a second time. Not that I seek or am eager for (your) gift, but I do seek and am eager for the fruit which increases to your credit (the harvest of blessing that is accumulating to your account).

But I have (your full payment) and more; I have everything I need and am amply supplied, now that I have received from Epaphroditus the gifts you sent me. (They are the) fragrant odor of an offering and sacrifice which God welcomes and in which He delights.

Philippians 4:15-18 (Amplified)

I thought people would have fallen over backwards to support the ministry of the great Apostle Paul. I thought they would have done everything in their power to help him. The Philippians were faithful to the ministry. This Scripture is talking about having a debit and credit account — giving and receiving in the financial realm.

Did you know that you can have a heavenly bank account? Many people want to withdraw from what they have in heaven, but they are overdrawn. They have been living off heaven's grace. You need to replenish your heavenly account and sow into eternity. The promised blessings of Philippians 4:19 only belong to believers who are faithful in supporting the work of the ministry.

The Traveling Ministry

In the early days of my ministry, I would call up a pastor and tell him we were passing through town and he would say, "Wonderful, just keep passing through." Then, if I did get a place to speak, they would give me a love offering — plenty of love and no offering. You needed a magnifying glass to find it. We once preached an entire week in the church of a millionaire farmer. We stayed in his home and when we departed they gave us a box of asparagus. They said, "God bless you, we really appreciate your ministry." Unfortunately, asparagus wouldn't pay for anything we may have needed.

Paul was a pioneer in more ways than one. First of all, he wrote two thirds of the New Testament. Then, he began a traveling ministry. Back then, they were not taught to support traveling ministries. Through the years, the traveling ministry has always been in conflict with the local church. Pastors have felt that the evangelists have come to take their money. Generally, a proper agreement has not been worked out — the evangelist does his thing and the church does its thing, which often leads to hard feelings.

For this reason, when we come as traveling evangelists, we pray that the church will be blessed because we are there. We believe for the church's income to go up. Many times, after four weeks of revival, the church receives the biggest Sunday offering they have ever had.

I am sharing this principle with you to help you understand what God expects from us. Stewardship is an important part of your Christian walk. If you want to be blessed of God, you need to be a good steward of your money.

Don't tell me, "I am not worried about money." Just wait until you have to feed your children. Then you start thinking, "Where can I get a couple of dollars?" Do you realize how much it costs to take care of a family? Have you found out that stores don't give anything away? Yet, people expect the gospel to be that way. Well, the Gospel is free, but it takes finances to get the Gospel out.

The Bible says in Proverbs 13:22 that the wealth of the sinner is laid up for the just. If you are faithful with the little, He will make you ruler over much. (Matt. 25:21.) Let me tell you why it is important to give. The apostle Paul said, **Not that I**

seek the gift, but I seek the fruit that abounds to your account. You need to give so that you may have fruit that abounds to your heavenly account.

You would never invest in a company that is going to fail or a business opportunity that is going to go bankrupt. Likewise, with the finances you plant for the work of God, invest in a ministry that brings forth fruit. Invest in a ministry that is going to produce successful outcomes for the kingdom of God.

Giving based on the Word of God will produce results in your life. Giving based on emotions will fade into nothingness. It will only give you temporary satisfaction. As you sow your finances into the work of God, purpose in your heart to sow in good soil. Tell the Lord, "Father, I'm sowing into good soil. I am investing in revival in America. I am claiming souls for Your kingdom. I am claiming that churches be revived and cities shaken by the power of God." Then you can expect a harvest. You can expect to reap in every soul that is saved.

Commit yourself today to take God at His Word and become a giver. His promises are true. Together, as faithful stewards, we can reach this world for Jesus and see His vision fulfilled.

Other books by Rodney Howard-Browne

Flowing in the Holy Ghost
The Touch of God
Manifesting the Holy Ghost
The Reality of the Person of the Holy Spirit
Fresh Oil From Heaven
The Anointing
The Coming Revival
Walking in the Perfect Will of God
What it Means To Be Born Again

To contact the author, write:

Rodney M. Howard-Browne
P.O. Box 197161
Louisville, KY 40259-7161